Letters from the Front

Extracts from letters sent to
Lt-Col Fane during the 1914-18 war

Julian F Fane

ISBN No: 978.1.903172.69.8

Publishers: Barny Books
              Hough on the Hill,
              Grantham,
              Lincolnshire
              NG32 2BB

              Tel: 01400 250246
              www.barnybooks.biz

FOREWORD

This interesting and eclectic collection of letters from the Western front of the first World War, the property of Mr Julian Fane of Fulbeck Manor in Lincolnshire, has recently come to light. They were written to Mr Fane's grandfather, Lieutenant Colonel William Fan of Fulbeck Hall, a veteran of the Boer War who was recalled to the Colours in 1914 to command the 3rd Reserve Battalion of the Lincolnshire Regiment which was responsible (among other duties) for the basic training of recruits for the Lincolnshire Regiment at Weelsby Camp near Grimsby. Lt Col Fane, by now too old to be sent to the front himself, was a caring and benign officer who had a deep interest in the men he trained and asked many of them to keep in touch with him after they joined their units on active service. Mr Fane has sifted through a large number of letters and selected a number which give a vivid picture of many aspects of life at the sharp end.

The immediate reaction is the, by now familiar to us all, horror at the conditions under which they lived and fought (many within yards of the enemy) – the mud, the sweat and the toil; the daily threat of being attacked (and themselves attacking); of being shelled and gassed by day and by night; the physical demands of digging miles of trenches; marching mile upon mile day after day, frequently to no great effect; feeling, on occasions, a lack of leadership from on high.

And yet, under all those fears and privations, there comes a spirit of comradeship and camaraderie which is endemic in the British soldiery. A feeling of loyalty, trust and friendship at all levels that over comes the temporal wretchedness of constant danger and discomfort. Many letters are understandably emotional in reassuring their families and friends of their concern for each other. It is nothing less than astonishing that the fundamental qualities of that whole generation were able to sustain an amazingly high state of moral during four years of unspeakable slaughter.

This issue is now part of the teaching curriculum in schools and this publication will be a useful reference to put across the feelings of those who took part in that dreadful experience between 1914 and 1918.

WE MUST REMEMBER THEM

Major General Richard E J Gerrard-Wright. CB CBE DL

Preface

Lt-Col William VR King-Fane.
Born 29 Oct 1868, died 5 Nov 1943

My grandfather was brought up at Melbourne Hall in Derbyshire. His side of the family moved to Fulbeck Hall in 1887 when his father bought Fulbeck Estate from his cousin. After reading law at Trinity College, Cambridge, he became a barrister. However, wars filled some twelve years of his life.

He fought in the Boar war in the Lincolnshire Regiment. Then in 1914 he was too old to take an active roll in the final front but commanded a Battalion of the Lincoln Regiment at Grimsby. This Battalion served as a training Battalion so almost all the Lincolnshire men who served during the 1914-18 war started at Grimsby before going to France and the front line. He was always interested to hear how these men were getting on and asked them to write to him with views and suggestions about equipment and training which would help them in France. From these letters are drawn this collection. A fascinating and often sad everyday reflections on life in the trenches.

His final war was when Fulbeck Hall was requisitioned in 1939 by the war office. He moved with his wife to the George Hotel in Grantham, leaving his home for Military use. In 1944, many of the plans for "Operation Market Garden", the battle of Arnhem, were worked out in Fulbeck.

Sadly, he did not live to see peace in 1945 but would have been very proud of his beloved County Regiment becoming the Royal Lincolnshire Regiment in 1946.

Julian Fane

Lt-Col William VR King-Fane

We have been through terrible times of late and now, all that remains of the old 1st Battalion are the Colonel, Masters and myself and five children of the Special Reserve.

We had a bad time last Sunday, for they sent us up in the dark to take a village that the Germans had driven our cavalry out of. We didn't know the country, or what we were up against, all they said was, "go on," and we went. There was a railway cutting on our side of the village and first of all we got into that. We hadn't been there a minute when we were fired on by what we took to be our own native troops so we did not return the fire but called out that we were English. They fired again and we returned it and I distinctly heard someone call 'tiro' in Hindustani, "you are firing on your own troops." We ceased fire again and the cursed Germans, for so they turned out to be, got into the cutting on the right and fired down it.

Three times we sent messengers back to ask for help and to stop the guns. The first two were killed before they had gone fifty yards and the third got through although he was hit twice and dragged himself back nearly two miles to the Colonel.

We went into action with 590 and there were 175 when I counted them. Every regular officer was killed or wounded.

F. Blackwood

From Captain Rich
No 2 Camp Sauric,
Havre.

14th November, 1914

My Dear Fane,
Just a line to tell you that we arrived safely. I saw nothing of the Yorkshires of Milnes and Jarvis, so I stuck to our draft and am commanding them so far without being deposed. The camp is a quagmire and it rained as I have seldom seen it rain before last night. It is damnably cold but nothing to what, no doubt, it will be. It's a very long way to this camp especially as with the usual staff arrangements, we were marched to No.3 camp and had to retrace our steps about three miles, all the journey in rain so that the men were soaked before we waded to the tents and when one man came up and complained that he had no sugar in his tea which had taken me three hours to collect at all, I was somewhat fed up and expressed my feelings somewhat forcibly.

I'm trying to get the men great coats instead of Macintoshes because I think they will be very cold up at the front in their rain coats. There seems to be a very large quantity of coats at the ordnance stores.

I collected a nice lot of tobacco with the £2 you gave me. We had a fairly quiet passage and disembarked about nine o'clock on Friday afternoon, not leaving Southampton until five o'clock on Thursday afternoon.

James and Robertson are here, both very anxious to go to the regiment, but the adjutant here, Wake, a man I know, they seem to send fellows to any regiment regardless of the corps they belong to. I shall stick to the draft until I'm forced out. Love to the others. I'll write when I can.

Yours Chas Rich

....

1st Lincolnshire Regiment. 2nd Army Corps. 3rd Division.
British Expeditionary Force.

22nd November, 1914

My Dear Fane,

I have arrived here with the Regiment coming with Tatchell and Jarvis. When I left Grimsby and arrived at Southampton, the transport officer told me that he knew nothing about the Yorkshire draft. I asked him what was best to do and he sent me with our draft to report at Havre. I remained with the draft up at the camp until I was ordered to join the Yorkshires which was arriving on Sunday.

I went to Headquarters, explained matters and said I should much prefer to go with the Lincolnshire regiment to which I belonged and they cancelled the Yorkshire order and told me to remain with the draft. I took the order to the C.O. Yorkshires and was ordered to proceed to join the Regiment with James and half the men. I left the other half behind with Owen, Robertson and Newberry. When we got to the 2nd Army Corps, I caught up with Tatchell and we joined forces. The C.O. here is also Blackwood, Black, Ricketts, Tugleby, a Captain of the Cameroons. The C.O. was delighted that we had come and will, if possible, get Milnes back. He inspected the draft this morning and said they were a more useful looking lot than the last. He complains that they couldn't handle their rifles. They could shoot straight, some of them but it's rapid fire that is required. When being attacked, they don't get off their rifles quick enough. It's the continuous fire that tells against the hordes of Germans.

The artillery and fire is continuous all day, whole batteries seemingly going off simultaneously.

It will be awful for the poor devils if we cannot get them great coats and boots. Many of the boots are shocking and the Macintosh coats worse than useless to keep the cold out. It is criminal sending men in these coats for a winter campaign. There are no coats at Havre. I spent hours at the Ordnance store and drew all I could. I drew some boots but Tatchell's lot have never had time to draw anything being sent out always just before he could get the things.

It's awfully cold here and the frost seems to get into every corner. The only thing for ones feet is to get a pair of boots about two sizes too big and wear socks. I have three pairs of socks on at the present time, two vests and two shirts, two pairs of drawers and anything else I can chuck on.

I hope the men will give a good account of themselves. Ingleby told me the other day he had to advance under fire. He whistled and signalled the advance and went on himself but nobody else followed. He had to stand up under fire and shout to the man to come on and then there was not much dash in it.

Anyway loading and firing quickly is the thing that is important. The German trenches are within 12 or 16 yards of ours so shelling is at present somewhat of a difficulty on both sides.

With many salaams to you and the few remaining pals I know,

Yrs ever Chas E. Rich.

....

7th Lincolns.
Lulworth Camp,
Dorset

22nd November, 1914

My Dear Fane,
I suppose you heard all about the regiment on 1st November. They lost between 350 and 400 men out of 600 and all the officers except five and the worst of it was that they had taken the village the previous day with little loss and were in full

possession, then they were ordered to retire without being attacked. John says they simply formed out and marched out and then, a few hours later after the Germans had come in and entrenched themselves, the Lincolns were ordered to retake it!

They advanced at 2a.m. and got as close as they could and then waited for dawn and charged but half of us were simply blown away. They got within about 75 yards and then lay there in a grip in the ground until the Colonel gave the orders to retire about mid-day. However they were greatly thanked by the Divisional General and the Brigadier for having saved the position by their prolonged stand. Tollemache was shot through the head and John thinks killed. Barlow was wounded and left on the ground and afterwards someone came to him and said a Major in the Lincolns was lying bayonetted, so John thinks he must have been killed while lying wounded.

Yours H.J.Jarr

....

1st Lincolnshire Regiment
2nd Army Corps,
3rd Division, B,E.F.

5th December, 1914

My Dear Fane,

I was awfully glad to get your letter. Of course I was only too anxious to get to the Regt. without actually going contrary to instructions. So, when I saw the opportunity, I took it.

We are in reserve until tomorrow at Loere. My billet is on the top of high hill. From it we get an extraordinary view of the battlefield or a portion of it, I should think some 30 miles or more. I can see Ypres away to the right and a great deal further NW of that away towards Messines.

We had some very unpleasant trenches last week and I believe we return to Nieus some time tomorrow but D Company which is mine (I always get D Co)) were on the right of the Regt and we had two poisonous trenches, mostly full of mud, water and dead French men. Thank goodness I move on to the left this time. I have covered places for the men this time. The others had no sort of protection.

We engaged the Germans at 6.15.a.m. on Monday morning whilst the French on our left attacked a very strong position but it didn't come off as the Germans had machine guns and the first line of French men hit the dust before they had advanced 100 yards so they returned to their former position.

We were about 150 yards from the German lines. I think we had about 6 casualties. Bloomfield of my draft was hit through the head also Corporal Cohen who has been here some time and 2 others wounded with my lot.

Another important thing in the trenches is keeping bolts and chambers of the rifles clean, also ammunition. The dirt and filth gets into everything and rifles are always jamming and becoming useless owing to bits of grit getting into the chambers. The men try to force the bolt back, sometimes with their feet – the extractor breaks and the rifle is rendered useless. Men have to get into the habit of continually oiling and wiping out chambers. At night, bayonets are fixed and this, too, is most important for the bayonet gets dirty from the trench and won't fix properly.

The main thing is discipline. Half the men (and the old soldiers are worse than the reserve men) haven't any idea of doing what they are told at once, consequently, when an advance is ordered, half the company remain. They have no habit of discipline.

A man was shot in the machine gun trench the other day, Sunday. I think 2 of the others (I brought some out) practically refused to come out and fire the guns. If I had been there, I swear I would have shot the first one that refused. I don't think you can represent it too strongly at Grimsby that the right sense of discipline is required here. I saw several old soldiers, re-enlisted men who went through S.A. with the 2nd Batt who, when the Germans fired, not at us, were firing their rifles over the top of the trench holding them above their heads so that they hadn't the smallest idea whether they were firing over the trees or into the ground.

I am telling you all this as I know you like to hear everything and I am so awfully anxious that the tremendous reputation of the Regt should not be impaired.

The King came to see us the other day and gave medals to some of the live and unwounded. The Regt has earned something like a dozen. There are a lot of good men in the drafts and if they only never questioned an order they'd be alright but some of them only think of their blasted skins.

Old Boxer has been rolled up as second in command. The C.O. is a topper and one feels one could do anything for him. Tatchell looks beastly but carries on. Fortie of the West Yorks came yesterday and has gone today sickening with rheumatic fever. Black is away sick and so is Captain Sword of the Scottish Rifles. We now have some 600 men.

Yrs ever

Chas Rich.

....

1st Lincolnshire Regiment,
B.E.F.

30. December, 1914

My Dear Fane,

I expect you have heard some of our news from Tatchell.

My wife went to see James in hospital. She also went to see a man who came out with me in Charing Cross Hospital, Thompson or Gibson, I can't remember which at the moment.

Anyway, he was a great runner and he got two frost bitten toes in the trenches.

We were lucky to get out of the trenches on Christmas Eve and we go back again tomorrow. We got a confidential from the G.O.C. (Smith Dorrien) saying that the Regiments didn't take enough trouble to improve the trenches when in them. Some regiments worked hard and it wasn't fair on those who did that they should find their trenches as bad as ever when they returned. The letter ended, the 1st Lincolnshires and the 1st Northumberland Fusiliers always improved their trenches. Irish Rifles are notable examples of the other way. I have Parish and Holton with me as subalterns now, the former is a most curious specimen but he works hard.

You will be glad to hear that many of the men are coming along well. We have still a number of those who don't intend to get into any danger if they can avoid it and, until they shoot a few Germans, they will never stop it.

Court martials have done their best but, in most cases, the powers commute the sentence and these would rather go to prison and be out of it rather than face German bullets. I notice that two or three of these men are those that egged you to send them out. Cunningham is one awaiting trial now. Bee is another. He was told to go up from support trenches and carry the equipment of a wounded man out and back one night when we were being relieved. His reply was, "I'm bl***** well not going up there, it's too f******(begging your pardon) dangerous." He has been tried but not promulgated yet.

Several of the S.A. heroes find it a very different game to the Boer War and don't like the change. Cunningham (of A) did a retirement of his own when the company was advancing and was brought back under escort, after 23 days saying he had lost the Regiment and couldn't find it again.

Like you, we suffer from a dearth of N.C.O.s. They are mostly young and inexperienced. They try and mean well but they have been Tom, Dick or Harry to the soldiers up to now. It's difficult to get a man to do some dirty job when ordered by that man who is now an N.C.O.. Officers are all very young too. There is nothing hardly out of their teens after the C.O., Boxer and myself.

I have certainly come to the conclusion that discipline is almost the most essential. We know that musketry is also absolutely necessary but, if only one could depend on men doing what they are ordered to do at once and with willingness born of discipline, it would be three quarters of the battle.

We are practising bomb throwing and shooting but, like everything else, we copy from the Germans. The Germans fire hundreds of star shells every night and they light up the whole of the immediate front. It's very difficult for any one man let alone a group to get far without being spotted.

I was out one night hunting for a trench that the Scottish were digging on our left as I was supposed to sap out from my left trench and meet up with them. I didn't know where their digging was taking place and, after some three and a half-hour crawl (with Sleight, my servant, an excellent man) we found that the covering sentries had been posted to the rear of the trenches. It wasn't surprising that, at one point, we found ourselves only fifteen yards from the German trenches. We could hear them speaking quite plainly. They dropped a star shell within a yard of us and we remained face downwards in eight inches of mud. When it did go out, I offered it at 40 miles an hour. Sleight remained until the small fusilade we caused had ceased.

I was awfully sorry to see about the poor little door-mouse. I wrote to his mother yesterday. Poor Wade's was a short lived promotion. I never even saw him.

Give all I know my love and best wishes for 1915.

Yrs very sincerely,
Chas E.F. Rich.

1st S.W,B.
1st Division

2nd January 1915

Dear Col. Fane,

I was lucky enough to be sent with a draft from Havre last Monday and so didn't waste much time at the base. We had 24 hours in the train and then marched 8 miles and joined the Regiment in billets about a mile behind our trenches.

At present the battalion takes 48 hours in the trenches and 48 hours in reserve. Half the battalion occupies the trenches while the other half in support is billeted in the houses about a quarter of a mile behind. This is possible because the German guns are very quiet as a rule. Our trenches are about 200-300 yards from theirs. We enter or leave the trenches by night and even then we lose a man or two as their snipers are very good, in fact about all our losses are from snipers or stray bullets. Their snipers crawl round behind our trenches and have an unpleasant way of potting officers. They have killed two of ours this week.

Owen was killed in an attack. I was very much disappointed to hear about it on arriving here. He was in this company and now a 2nd Lieutenant of four months service commands us and I am the only other officer in the company.

Yours very sincerely,
J.F.Neilson

....

1st Lincolnshire Regiment,
2nd Army Corps,
3rd Division.

My dear Fane,

It may help you a bit if I tell you what I have found best for the trenches in the way of clothes etc. In the first place I recommend Lotus boots. They are practically watertight. You want them ample. I wear three pairs of thick socks. I put my putties on before my boots and have a pair of anklets over both. This keeps the water out of the top of your boots better than anything else.

Cod liver oil is very good to rub into your feet well before putting on your socks, it prevents frostbite. You want very thick drawers and vest and shirt, a good cholera belt and a couple of Jaeger linings loose to put into breeches is very useful, one on and one off. Gum boots are quite essential out of the trenches but I don't recommend them for the trenches themselves. Personally I don't believe in a great coat. They are too long and not a loose enough style of garment.

A British Warm to come just over the knees and a loose Burberry that will slip on easily over the top is best. A Sam Browne belt is useful to have to wear when in billets but Tommy's equipment is best for the trenches.

Yours sincerely,

Chas. E.F. Rich

. . . .

Weelsby Camp 1916

2nd Lincolnshire Regiment,
No 16 Camp,
Havre.

22nd February, 1914

Sir,

We sailed from Southampton at daybreak on Saturday and arrived at Havre about 1.30. We only saw one German seaplane and that was just after leaving the Isle of Wight but it did not molest us.

There were about 150 British officers and several Belgian officers and men. Most had adopted webbing equipment and only one, a Seaforth, had brought out a sword.

The men here only number 12, some of whom were sent back from Grimsby and all have been wounded or sick in French hospitals. There were about fifty last week but, on Saturday, those that were fit went to the battalion.

I think we all feel as if we are on a holiday or picnic but certainly not in active service.

We have a mess here where our rations are cooked and we ourselves add three francs a day.

I remain, Sir, yours sincerely,

G,L,Marshall

....

Dear Colonel Fane,

We arrived at Southampton at 2p.m. but did not sail until the following day. On arrival at Havre we were shut up in a huge shed for thirty hours to await transport to take us to Rouen. I got rid of my draft there and was sent out with twenty men to the 1st Batt. I found Captain Jarvis there also Disbourne and Robertson. I found the battalion in billets. They had just had an awful three days in the trenches and everybody was fed up. The trenches were half full of water and only 80 - 150 yards from the Germans. Some of the men had to be lifted out when they were relieved and nearly all were suffering from rheumatism, pains in the back, etc. The battalion was ordered to attack one night and lost rather heavily. Poor Wade was probably killed as he is missing and his hat was found with bullet holes in it. Captain Tatchell was hit through his right fore-arm. James was also hit in his back and leg. The attack was a failure as the enemy were in force and had three Maxim going against the attacking party. Of course I wasn't in this show myself but got the report from Newbury and Ingleby..

The three of us have rather a nice billet and are very comfortable. We hope to remain here for a while. Our brigade went into the trenches today but, fortunately, we are in reserve so stay in our billet. There are rumours that our division rests for a time soon. The battalion is 550 strong but some of the very old men are being sent back to the lines of communication. We have two officers to each of these companies but the others have one only. Major Boxer from 2nd Batt is in command and Ricketts is doing adjutant. Artillery is firing practically all day. One big gun near us shakes the house every time it goes off,

I am, Sir, Yrs faithfully,
G.W. Harriss. 2nd Lieut. Lincs Regt.

…………………

Rouen   1 Dec. 1914

My Dear Colonel,
Just a line to let you know the news.
When we reached Havre, an old Scots Reserve Major who has been living in Canada for the last 12 years and one or two other young officers took up 500 men straight away and left me with the 350 balance to march up to camp and such a camp with about four inches of slush and mud everywhere. Then I was given some of the S.Wales Borderers to command, the Yorks being handed on to a fellow in the Scots Fusiliers. Now I am officially in the 2/Bedfords, not knowing a soul in the mess.
Newbury is a major in the E.Yorks. They left for the front last night. I think they had 190 men, they were all in great spirits. I was very lucky to catch them as they marched down.
I have been talking to fellows who have come down from the front. They tell me that trenches are generally dug to hold three men and you begin them at night. If you haven't dug down to 4 feet by day break, you don't stand a chance from the shells.
Hands get just like navvies' hands from the digging and the dirt becomes ingrained. After getting down to 4 feet, you then make the communication trenches. You also need to have a small parapet to the rear to protect from the blow back of exploding shells.
A lot of men have come down with rheumatism, quite bent, and a good number of frost bites.

There is a splendid ordnance depot at Havre where the men are marched down and given any clothing and equipment they need on the signature of an officer. Things have been rather difficult up to now but stuff is coming up fast. Rations are excellent. The men get one and a quarter pounds of fresh meat, bread, jam, cheese, butter, bacon daily and 2 ozs of Capstan weekly. Rum is only served to them at the front so they have nothing to complain about.

Our Tommies call Ypres, Wipers. They are undefeatable at French but they get on very well with the natives.

Please remember me to your wife,

Yrs ever,

C.F.C.Jarvis..

....

May 2nd, 1915.
Convalescent Camp,
Rouen.

Dear Col,

I must apologize for not writing to you before to thank you for all your kindness while I was attached to the Lincolns. I was sent to base hospital when I came out and from there was transferred to this camp a fortnight ago.

The hospitals here are splendid, beautifully equipped with every convenience. They are all built in huts about half the size of the huts used at home and can take about 100. We usually admit three or four hundred a day and send on about the same number to their various bases.

I am leading a life of ease and idleness compared with my work in Grimsby and wish that I had more to do.

I was sorry to hear that the measles are still flourishing there but I expect they will soon die out.

I've met several of the Lincolns since I came out and I was jolly glad to see them and have a chat about old times. I came up from Havre with Greatwood and Hutchinson and have met Jarvis, Herepath, Skelly, Marshall and Fairbrother here. I met Robertson yesterday. He had come to the camp to bring a draft of convalescents. I was awfully pleased to see him as I hadn't met him since his first time home. I also met some of the men as they occasionally come to this camp from hospital. I expect I'll see a good many more of them when they have been in the next big fight. Poor chaps, they are all wonderfully cheerful and they would all give a lot to get home for a while.

Everybody here is very optimistic that the war will be over in a few months but I fail to see how they come to that conclusion.

I am, yours sincerely,

Stanley P. Stokes

. . . .

The Welsh Hospital, Netley.

18 May, 1915

My Dear Colonel,

I arrived here today from France with a broken leg, an accident. I had been round the trenches and was returning to my trench. It was raining and had been raining all day so the ground was slippery. I jumped an old trench and slipped on landing and sat on my left foot dislocating it and breaking a small bone. I was quite close to my trench so the stretcher bearers didn't take long to find me and took me down to the dressing station. While the doctor was dressing me, another ambulance arrived and I was sent out at once to hospital from where I was, next morning, sent on to the railhead. The train was full of casualties of Thursday's fight and all cavalry who suffered mainly from the German artillery fire. That Friday evening we were at Boulogne and were sent on from there to Versailles arriving on Saturday morning. That is the No. 4 General Hospital and is in the Trianon Palace Hotel. It is a beautiful hospital. A large number of us were drafted off yesterday morning to Rouen.

On Sunday afternoon, Ingoldsby arrived. He had been sent down sick from the 5th Batt. suffering from gastric influenza.

This hospital is in the rear of the main building of the big hospital. I hear that Griffiths is in the main building.

To go back to my departure from Grimsby. The passage was bad and the ship very crowded. I found it quite impossible to remain below so I got hold of a bit of sail cloth and climbed into one of the life boats and slept well there. We waited at Havre for a few hours for the tide and then went up to Rouen. The river journey was very pretty. I got into camp about 3 o'clock, that was No. 5 Base camp and then was transferred to our own depot, No 3. I was there two days and then had to take up a draft of our men, partly convalescents and the rest Johnson's. Johnson had to take a draft of the Rifle Brigade by the same train. The march to the station was in heavy rain and the entrainment was in a deluge but the men were all very cheery. There must have been 4,000 on that train. The next morning, somewhere near Boulogne, the train began to leave portions cut off for the different railheads. We were then put on motorbuses and taken a considerable way. We then had half an hour's march to where Regt No.2 stores were. We moved out after dark that evening and, after slow and devious ways, we reached the **sot(?)** we had been told to go to. The following night, the draft moved out and joined their companies. My company was in the trenches and I found Cave Orme there. The other subalterns were Trazier and Green (from the artists) and Perkins.

We came out of the trenches on the 4th night. Perkins was so bad with the fever that he had to be carried down to the dressing station and he and Parrish (also fever) were sent off that night, both bad cases. I was in reserve for 4 nights and then 130 men joined from the Base Depot. One lad was wounded on the way up, Pte Colvill. The night before I went into the trenches again, Jeudwine was injured. It was my second night in the trenches that I broke my leg.

I saw poor Grantham's grave. The men of his company are very good in the way they look after it whenever the company comes out of the trenches.

A youngster named Teversham attached to No.2 Batt came across with me and is here now. He broke a finger playing football.

Please excuse the scrawl. I am not accustomed to writing in bed,

Yrs sincerely,
H.M.C.Orr

………………………………

Billets at Westontie.
December 7th 1915

Dear Colonel,

I thought you might like a line from me to know how we are getting on. The battalion is now roughly 400 strong with about a fighting strength of 300. I suppose you have heard that poor Ingoldsby was badly hurt on the 3rd. He was my company officer and we had just finished breakfast when he stood up to stretch in our little shelter in the trench when he was hit in the shoulder by a sniper before he had even straightened himself up. I didn't think it was serious although he was in great pain all day but the doctors say it has pierced his lung. He is doing very well however and left the hospital for the base today. Of course, he had to lie in the trench all day and it was a rotten day as the Germans shelled us. Seven 'Jack Johnsons' dropped within twenty yards of us without hitting the trench or injuring anybody but they covered us with mud every time. That was the first time I had been under shell fire as the German guns have been remarkably quiet until the last few days. Our guns often pounded the German trenches in front of us for hours at a time and absolutely knocked them to bits.

We often hear the Germans shout and once we saw a German go flying up in the air. Everything is pretty quiet here. There seems little possibility of an advance. There are continual rumours that our division is to be relieved and have a rest but they never seem to come to anything. When we went into the trenches last time, we were told that we were to do four days instead of three and we would have 8 days rest. When we got out, we were told that the 8th brigade had gone to relieve the French and we would only have four days rest and then go back to the trenches. So we will be in again tomorrow. The trench I was in last time had no traverses and was enfiladed. It was nearly, in all parts, a foot deep in mud and water. It was 6-8 feet wide and the parapet was practically non-existent. We generally work all night trying to improve the trenches but the ground is so awful that if you dig mud out, it simply slips back again and, after a few hours rain, a very common occurrence here, the greater part of the parapet and excavated earth finds its way back into the trench which seems to act as a sort of drain for the district.

Skelby came up here on the 2nd and after one day in the trenches went sick and has been sent off today.

Could you tell me how it is that Disabrowe and I have not been confirmed in our rank? We both have Certificate B, O.T.C. and were only required to do three months probationary period so we should have been confirmed ages ago.

Yrs etc,

J.A.Harris,   2nd Lieut. 1st Lincolns Regt.

Nov 24, 1914.

Dear Colonel,

    I suppose you have heard what bad luck poor old Lisle had. The battalion was lying in reserve on a road and about three stray bullets came over and the only fellow that was hit was Lisle who was killed practically at once. It was pitch dark at the time.

    Bromhead went sick with ague or something about five days after he joined and Dove went sick about a fortnight after he joined. He looked pretty bad and had lost a lot of weight. Wasn't it sad about King and Brausbury. They were both killed after I left so I can't tell you what happened. I got my bit of shrapnel on Oct. 20th. It went in at the top of my shoulder and is still somewhere in my rib area. So far, they have failed to get it out. I have had a pretty rotten time as the wound was very septic but I hope to get out of hospital in early December unless I have to have another operation.

I hope you are not having too bad a time. I can't think of anything worse than sleeping on Grimsby shore with that terrible smell.

The 1st Batt have, I think, only one of the original lot left – in addition to the fellows that joined from your Batt. Major Barlow and three York and Lancaster officers attached have been knocked out. It really is dreadful.

By the way, I saw an Oct. Army list and find that I am bottom but one of the 2nd Lieutenants. All the fellows that joined after me have been put above me. I sent in my first application the day the war broke out and then applied to the Depot in Lincoln so I suppose I ought to have been gazetted before Aug 20th which is the date put down on the Army List. I don't want to give you any trouble so please don't take any notice if it is going to cause you worry.

Yrs sincerely,
R.H.Spooner.

. . . .

Restaurant Tortons, Havre.

8th June, 1915.

Dear Colonel Fane,

I thought that you might like to know that I shall be at the base camp for a day or two. The draft of 30 men that you sent out here yesterday arrived safely and are short of nothing. Route marches and musketry are the main parades. Some trenches and barricades with loop holes have been set up and fellows practice rapid firing with live ammunition.

Some of the men in other Regs are very badly trained. One man in the Leicesters tried to load a rifle by putting the bullet end of his cartridge straight down into the magazine. Another fellow in the Liverpools had no idea how to fix a bayonet on. I think our fellows take a high place.

We have had no excitement so far except that a couple of spies were caught in camp yesterday, one was a German.

Yrs. Sincerely,
R.H. Spooner.

…………………….
24th June, 1915.

My Dear Colonel – I am writing this to tell you that I am engaged to Miss Stephens at Gt. Coates. Do you know them? I wasn't quite engaged before I left but am most awfully glad that it is settled now.

We had an attack 8 days ago (Wed) and we got a good many of their trenches but had to give up some of them as our own artillery wouldn't stop shelling them. Then the Wilts gave up their trench on our right and went back because the Germans sent a bombing party down the trench from the right. This was a great pity as their trench enfiladed the front of the others and was a very important one. And then, that night, we had to give up another on account of this but still held the ones in front of Y wood which we still hold. Since then, we have had two days rest which meant reorganising as we lost 50 per cent of our officers and men. And then we came to these trenches, again on the right of the place we attacked. 3 companies are in the firing line now- and one in support- and the men are tired.

You will have heard of the officer casualties. Since then, poor old Wickham has been killed in the trenches by a rifle grenade. No news has been heard of Major Boxer or Green, Walked or Pearson. I'm afraid there is very little hope for them. Green and Pearson are almost certainly killed.

The rest of the Brigade was equally cut up. The Liverpool Scottish (Territorials) lost all but 2 of their officers. They were a very fine Regiment indeed. Our artillery did awfully well in preparing the way for us again when we counterattacked. It was a pity though that they hadn't enough communications to stop when our attack went forward.

Yrs. Very sincerely ,
R.J. Johnstone.

……………………………

4th July 1915   2nd Batt, Lincs Regt.

Dear Colonel Fane,

Today is memorable for the presentation of the V.C. to Corporal Sharpe who thoroughly deserved it.

We were all very sorry to hear that Major Boxer is missing. He had only just left this Batt to join the 1st. Robertson who belongs to my company was taken prisoner while out on patrol a fortnight ago. The patrol was fired on and I'm afraid he must have been wounded. I only hope he was not killed. Another patrol went out to bring him in and shouted his name. The Germans replied, "alright, we have got him," so we must hope for the best.

No serious event has happened to 2nd Batt since I joined. I just missed the affair at Frinelles and I'm glad I did.

Barker is here and Rushton has been posted to my company to replace Robertson. The men are very cheerful and I rather think they prefer being in the trenches to being in billets. There are no parades in the trenches and they can cook meals at almost any time of the day. Having to be up all night doesn't seem to bother them at all.

Yesterday, Sunday, Corporal Sharpe was presented with the V.C. by the G.O.C. Division. He won it for great gallantry in bombing the enemy and holding them up in their trenches at Neuve Chapelle.

The billets we occupy vary in comfort. In my present billet, my room gives access to the front door and the daughters of the house frequently rush in and out. If they happen to catch me at my toilet, they are kind enough not to be offended. My bed, which is on the floor, is the daily resort of the household pets and my nights, in consequence, are somewhat disturbed.

I forgot to add that Sergeant Spittall who went out with Robertson carried back a wounded man first binding up his wound which was serious. Then he went out again with the 2nd patrol to look for Robertson.

A draft joined us two days ago which had been held up for some time at Havre, I don't recognise as many faces as I used to. No doubt most of the men I knew are all out.

I remain, Yrs sincerely,
W.A. Pitt

. . . .

In billets.   July 9th 1915.

Dear Colonel Fane,

I have been meaning to write to you ever since I landed here. I was so sorry to go away from Grimsby without seeing you. I particularly wanted to thank you for your kindness to me, not only while I was at Grimsby but also for admitting me to the Regiment at the start in spite of my age. I think it is unnecessary for me to tell you that I would not change for any other Regt in the army. I just had four days in the trenches and then the Batt came back here for a rest. It was a funny sensation to me the first time I was under fire but I was very lucky to be in such a good trench. The 5th Lincolns have got their band out here and they gave us a really excellent concert last Sunday which I think was much appreciated by all.

With kindest regards,

Yours sincerely,

Kenneth J. Edmondson

July 3rd

Dear Col. Fane,

I joined the first Batt here about a fortnight ago. They had just gone up to the trenches. Wickham was killed the 2nd evening. It was a most extraordinary piece of luck. He was walking down the trench when a rifle grenade pitched into the trench behind a traverse just as he was passing the place and burs within about a foot of him. I was two traverses up the trench and when I got there, he was unconscious and he only lived about a quarter of an hour.

Edmondson, Kirk and Disbrowe arrived last week and H. Marshall has also rejoined. Captain Tucker has brought his draft here and another draft is expected this evening so the company is getting quite strong. Boys and Hopper are away on five days leave. Others are also going including the N.C.O.s and men so we're hoping that we're going to have a jolly long rest. We are now in camp a good ten miles behind the trenches,

Yours sincerely,

D.F. Neilson.

. . . .

1st Lincolns,

July 25th 1915.   B,E. Force, France.

Dear Col. Fane,

I am at last up with the battalion. I was at Havre for 12 days and it was hard work while I was there, jobs like censoring. The pick of the bunch were jobs like kit inspection and parading the Division or jobs like trench digging, charging etc. A party of the Wilts were entrusted to me to bring up. We came up via Boulogne, Calais etc to Poperinge. Their billets were well over on the south side of the town, consequently didn't get over there until 11p.m. The following morning, I joined the battalion who are in dug outs in Reserve just north of Dickebusch.

We are in a small wood about 1600 yards from the firing line. There is a lot of construction work done by us and others just in front so we're not free from occasional shells. Cross roads on the edge of the wood are shelled regularly each afternoon, fortunately after our parties have withdrawn. We are expected to move soon, probably into billets. I hope so.

I'll now let you hear the news I've procured.

Major grant, C.O. and Capt Johnson, 2nd
Capt Littleton ......A Company (N staff)
Capt de Boys.......B Co
Capt Marshall......C Co.
Capt fenwick........D Co.
The subalterns are;
Lt. Disbrowe
Lt de la Motte
2/Lts Jacques and Rowland (both artists' rifles just joined)
2/Lt Edmondson.....B Co.
  " Scott (artists)
  "   Duncan and Rowale – Liverpool Scottish
  " Bruce
  " Bowen ....C Co.
  " Perkins   _3rd Devons Bombers.
  " Edes
  " Harris   Bedford Regt.
Lt. Hopper ..... D Co.
  " Neilson
2ndLt Churchhouse.....artillery ranker.
  " Kirk
Capt. Tucker   .. attached.

     I am pleased to say I'm with the machine gun section as 2nd string to Toupey attached to A Company. We've 4 guns and the majority of them were fellows that we had at Grimsby.

     Hutchinson was in charge of C Company but he's away ill, as are 2nd/Lt Sherman (bad ankle) and Parish of M.G. section and so is LT Skilly with a bad breakdown.

     I think that is all.

     We are having a lot of night work to do, continually taking lots of Kitchener's army fellows up to the trenches, fairly exciting,

With kindest regards,

Ys Sincerely, F, W. Clifton.

1st Lincs,
9th Brigade,
3rd Division.

July 3rd. 1915.

Dear Colonel Fane,

We are in clover behind the lines having a rest. I only had two days before we came here. At first the noise makes one very thoughtful, to put it mildly.

The men are grand and I'm proud to be with them. I hope I do my job half as well as they do theirs – an officer's job done well is a very great responsibility. We are well fed and looked after and the regular officers are as nice to us as they possibly could be. Hope the third is going strong,

G.A. Kirk.

H.M.S. Sir John Moore.
Aug 24th 1915.
c/o G.P.O.

My Dear Mother,

Here we are safe in harbour again and remarkably glad too. I daresay you have read about a certain liveliness in the North Sea which I daresay you guessed we had a hand in. You will also perhaps be able to guess which operation we carried out. The Admiral flew his flag in this ship and I had an anxious time piloting the whole squadron across and back. The Skipper and I have had about five hours sleep in the last seventy two hours so, today, we are just about worn out. I can't tell you much about the show except to say that we seem to have worried the Bosches. We had no casualties and were not attacked by aircraft.

The Admiral is very nice, which is lucky as I have a good deal to do with him in my capacity of fleet navigator but I don't think he remembered me as one of his midshipmen.

We are now having a rest which is rather necessary as the last 3 weeks have been absolute slave driving in preparation for the effort we have just made. However it's all extremely interesting. Between our operations (as now for instance), you need not worry about my safety as we take no risks. I might manage to get a day or two off soon if we go up river but all is uncertain these days,

Yr Loving son, Francis Lambert.

1st Lincolns,
B.E.F.
1st August 1915

Dear Col. Fane,

You've no doubt read in the papers an account of a German attack at Hooge. This occurred a couple of nights ago and, from the varied accounts we've received, Kitchener's army does not appear to be quite up to standard. The general report and one we put most faith in was that it started with this infernal liquid fire which forced the XIV Division to give way. This Division was holding those trenches we took on the 16th and you can quite imagine the disgust it has caused. They are a part of the new army and were utterly terrorized by the liquid fire and the trenches were easily captured. A relief had just been completed which the Germans were apparently aware of. One Battalion stuck to their line and lost heavily later in the day whilst the other was driven behind the Zouave Wood. Matters remained like this till the morning when we managed to drive the Germans back and have now fortunately regained all but two of the lost trenches. Last night, I believe the Huns massed behind their lines at that point and were spotted by one of our airmen. Our artillery were informed and did a bit of wonderful shooting and, it is stated, gave them shocks. I rather believe this for they didn't attack again. The Battalion of this new army that did the drawing back also lost heavily for they've only about 100 men and an officer left. Rather rotten.

The official report considers the liquid fire a bit of a failure for only three men were burnt. The moral effect must be pretty bad though.

We are to move from this wood this morning. When we received this notification, we made sure we were for Hooge but now find out that we're to go about a mile and a half N W of it near Polezzi which is where the trenches are that we are to occupy and they're about 300 yards apart, loop hole trenches I'm told but supports are badly shelled daily. We are no doubt in for it now but hope it'll not be for long. Edes has left us pro tem to train as a mining officer. He is to be away for about a week.

I see from the casualty list that Ross is hit, not badly, I hope. Rather unfortunate for the Adj because Ross will probably want his bike back now.

Masters tells me that the 4th Batt has been knocked about and he thinks they were round about Hooge. You'll be pleased to know that I find the machine gunners from Grimsby far superior in general efficiency than those already out here. Others also remark this but in gun pit construction they are not so good. There is a lot of this to be done out here.

With kindest regard

I remain,

Yours sincerely,

F.W. Clifton

No 3 Infantry Base Depot,
B.E. Force

1st August 1915

Dear Col,

We got pushed on here from Havre straight away being posted to the No 6 Entrenching Batt. It is made up from mainly 5 Div but some from here. There are in all about 1200 men from any quantity of different units. Luckily mine are all from the Manchester Regt but Wiseman has got men from 5 lots. We have a Colonel Atherton as C.O. for nothing else but the men. We are not likely to go up for another ten days or so. Nobody knows what our job is to be but the general opinion is that we are to get positions ready behind the line to save the Batts from the trenches a certain amount of work. Some say that we will pass the men on to their units and others say not. They are forming 8 or 10 of these stray lots between here and Havre. The men we have here are nearly all from the 9th and a few being out of the hospital here.

Yrs sincerely,
Anthony William Freeman.

. . . .

In the trenches
4 Aug 1915.

My Dear Colonel,

I saw General Smith last time we were out of the trenches and he said that we had only sent him one bad draft and expressed surprise at the number and quality of men that we had. In spite of the usual grouse or two about various things, I think the general opinion is highly complimentary. I thought you would like to hear this.

We have had very few changes lately. Ross was wounded slightly and Leslie has gone sick again. We are well up to strength again now. We are having a fairly quiet time but a lot more lively than last month but I expect that things will be very different in the future now that Warsaw has been evacuated.

Please remember me to all I knew at Grimsby.

Yrs very sincerely,

M. Barker.

....

Spilsby.

Dear Colonel Fane,

You will be sorry to hear that our boy has been hit again by a bullet or piece of a shell in his chest. The doctor said that it was a nasty wound but ought to be alright. Since beginning this letter we have had a wire from the War Office reporting him seriously ill yesterday and are feeling very anxious. They will report progress. He is in No 19 casualty clearing station Abeele.

Captain Littleton wrote a kind letter speaking very highly of him as one of the best subalterns he ever had and we also heard from Johnson with a message from Grant. The Chaplain also wrote from hospital so we feel grateful for all their kind thoughts. He was listed on Sunday just after writing to us from the trenches telling us about the whizz bangs that were bursting all around him.

Yours sincerely,

C.P. Disbrowe.

....

29 August 1915

Dear Colonel Fane,

Since writing to you last, the Batt has occupied 3 different parts of the line and is now in possession of an old position in Sanctuary Wood. We have been having a fairly quiet time on the whole and I suppose we should consider ourselves lucky though there is absolutely no sign that the Brigade is entitled to an appreciable rest.

You heard about poor old Disbrowe. I was with him immediately after he had been hit and had no idea he was so badly hurt. In fact, a gem of a stretcher bearer, Cresswell, chipped him on getting a Blighty. I saw him again at the hospital near Ypres and found him so much better that he was about to be sent back to England. No doubt he is there ere this.

This present line is a contrast to the one we held in Potinge for there, we were far apart and were treated to Whizz Bangs. Here, in places very close, rifle grenades are the order of the day.

You'll be sorry to hear that Impey has gone ill. He developed a temperature and was packed off to hospital. The Doctor considers it is nothing serious and believes it is a case of trench fever. Rather rotten luck though although if he gets to England he is to be envied. Fenwick has also gone ill with a species of itch.

We all had a pleasant surprise the other day by a visit from Cocks. He had lost himself after tramping for miles when he came upon us at a bivouac so, augmented by a few of us, we escorted him to his Battalion.

I shall close with kindest regards to you and the adjutant,
Yours sincerely,
F.W.Clifton.

....

August 17th 1915

My Dear Colonel,

We are out of the trenches for three days but go back to the centre of operations on Thursday. We had a month practically continuous and then these three days out. It's not a very long rest.

I was very sorry not to come over and see you when I got home last but I only got 3 days and I hadn't seen Miss Stephens since we got engaged. You have seen her now so she tells me so you can understand that I wanted as much time with her as I could get.

She enjoyed the sports very much indeed and told me about the bombing competition and the Tug of War. I would very much have liked to have been there myself.

We have just been playing football. I had a try myself and it was quite good fun but so slippery it was impossible to stand up. Rich has started a Divisional band and it played here yesterday afternoon. It is a good thing whilst we are in this trench stagnation business.

Young Disbrowe is rather bad. He is still in the Clearing Hospital. Boys went over to see him yesterday. He seemed cheerful but short of breath. I'm going to see him tomorrow.

These Zeppelin raids must be a great nuisance. Have they got any guns that will reach them near Grimsby or do they still dig trenches to ward them off.

I can't think why they don't mix up the territorial's and Kitchener's with the regulars. We could have a splendid Lincoln Brigade out here. It would level out the whole lot.

Yours very sincerely,
R.H. Johnstone.

....

A Company,
5th Entrenching Battery,
20th August 1915
B.E.F.

Sir,

Since I arrived in France, I have been moved about a good deal and was in charge for some time of a detachment unloading stores at the railhead. I have now joined the right half of the Batt and am in a position to inform you that we are engaged in felling trees and with the material obtained make pit props and stakes of all sizes from 1 foot to ten feet and hurdles etc. In fact everything of wood useful in field fortifications. When we arrived, Mr Baines and Mr Denning were sent to the left half of the Battery which is billeted about five miles away and although I have not heard from them, I believe they are engaged in the actual construction of trenches,

We are putting in 7 working days a week and have been congratulated on the work we have done,

I remain, Sir
Yours obediently,
S. Shankster.

14 September, 1915
1st Lincolns,
B.E.F.

Dear Sir

Have now joined the above Battalion and am having a little more varied experience. We are alternately occupying the trenches and having digging fatigues. The latter consist of constructing long communication trenches behind the lines. Unfortunately we have had two casualties from strays. I am in D Company under Captain Fenwick.

We had a visit from Frift and Sowerby the other day. They seem to have had rather a rough time while in the trenches.

Our operations are being kept secret for various reasons and every effort is made to conceal our work from the Huns. I am sorry not to be able to give you the particulars of our work but there is always the danger of a letter being lost in the post,

Yours sincerely,
S Shankster.

....

No 3 General Hospital,
Sep 6t. 1915
Le Treport.

Dear Colonel Fane,

I had no opportunity to present the letter to the D.A.G. that you kindly gave me. There were 290 officers on board the good ship on which we crossed, nearly all of these were sent to Territorial Battalions and it was a regular bear fight. We were like a lot of sardines in a box. I went to see the O.C. reinforcements Officer when I got to Honfleur Camp. I saw numerous people. They were very decent but could do nothing. We were in Havre four days and attended some splendid lectures. We were then sent to Rouen to the N. Midlands Division Base and were there one day before going up to the

45

front. We were attached to the 4th Division. They have done very well and have been managed splendidly. They seemed very pleased to see us, Captain Johnson having gone sick. Harrison was awfully seedy and, as soon as possible, he went into an Officers' Hospital at Havre with asthma. We left him being very well looked after. On going to billets, I was delighted to find the 1st quite close to us and saw my brother that evening. He turned up at the farmhouse where we were billeted with Neilson, Kirk and Clifton. I went for a long ride with him. The officers I saw all seemed to be in good form. I was awfully sorry to miss Toupey. He had gone sick with trench fever.

Well, Sir, I will tell you what I am doing here. Since the Germans greeted the Battalion with, 'Hello 4th Lincolns,' I am sure I can be giving away no secrets in saying we have been in trench 49 in just about the middle of the Ypres salient, a pretty warm corner. As you know, we have been giving them plenty of high explosives lately and shelling in general. They were tired of this and on Friday, in pouring rain with the trenches absolute quagmires, they proceeded from 2.15 until 2.45. to give our particular bit of the line a good straffing. This made an awful mess of the right half of our trench. They gave us whizz bangs, trench mortars, shrapnel, rifle grenades and machine gunfire. It was very warm indeed. It was just spite really and the affair was of a very concentrated nature. We had to give the battery covering us the S.O.S. signal. Only seven men and myself were wounded – all slightly. I have a shrapnel bullet or bit of shrapnel in my back just above the left buttock. They have X -rayed me this morning and will presumably remove it tomorrow. I am very fit myself.

My brother is now in command of 13 Company. He feels the responsibility very much. I have always regarded it as a great honour to be able to consider myself a member of the Battalion. I remain, Sir,

Yours very sincerely,
Neil Edmondson.

1st Lincolns, B.E.F,   27 Sept 1915

Dear Colonel Fane,

Just a few lines to let you know how we fared during this last Hooge affair.

We held the trenches to the immediate right of the crater for a week before the day and had a pretty hot time of it. All this area was continually shelled but we were very fortunate in having few casualties. On the first day, the 1st Gordons pushed off from the crater, 4th Gordons from the trenches we had been holding and the 1st Royal Scots from their right, augmented with a coupe of companies of the Scots Fusiliers. They all lost very heavily. The 1st Gordons were machine gunned fearfully and failed to take the first line trench. The 4th Gordons and the Scots took four lines but had to retire during the afternoon from a terrific bombing counter attack. During the attack, we were Divisional Reserve and were Whiz Banged badly from 10 a.m. in the morning till 8 at night. The shells were coming over at regular one minute intervals. Our Bombers reinforced the Scots and did jolly well. Sergeant Pashley of A Company was killed, a small crump which nearly did me in as it took away part of the dug out. We relieved the Scots that night and came out the following night after an absolutely quiet day.

Just after we had been relieved, a terrific artillery strafe took place and we had a rotten time getting away. They shelled the transport road but we got through O.K. In fact, this last week, we have had an extremely exciting time.

Can you tell me what happened to the crowd of fellows that joined the Batt in May, McTurk, Fairweather etc. Sippe and Ravula have joined us from the Suffolks.

With kindest regards to you and the adjutant,
Yours sincerely,
F.W.Clifton

47

8th Lincoln.
B.E.F.

Oct 7th 1015

Dear Sir,
Just a line to let you know that Fairweather, Duff and myself have arrived at this Battalion. Fairweather has been made machine gun officer. Duff, Preston and myself have each got a Company besides which I am bombing officer so we are pretty busy. All the officers here are awfully nice chaps.
With kind regards,
Yours sincerely,
F.w.Latham.

....

Ludshott House,
22nd May, 1915
Grayshott,
Hants.

My Dear Fane,
Many thanks for your letter. Rupert has had another very lucky escape. He was shot through the body near the right shoulder. The bullet went straight through without injuring any bone or artery or nerve. He, of course, lost a lot of blood. He was hit on the 10th, Sunday and was in a London Hospital on Tuesday night and came home on Monday last. The wounds are about healed but it has pulled him down a bit and he has to go slow, not feeling quite up to things yet. He goes before a medical board on Monday fortnight. He said the Germans had got to know about the attack (on Fromelle) and left their trenches during our preliminary bombardment and when we charged, they came back, he was hit after the first German line was taken. He

was sent out to catch a German sniper and the sniper got him first. The Batt had only one Maxim.

Glad to see that Fitz, Cox has got the command,

Yours very sincerely,
Charles J.E.Parker.

No 7 Stationary Hospital,
28th May 1915
Boulogne sur Mer

Dear Fane,

It is now expected that Rupert will make a good and eventually full recovery. At first it was thought his terrible wound was a mortal one but he pulled round better than was expected after the operation at Balleul and now he is going on quite satisfactorily so, barring complications, he is going to pull through. We were wired for on Sunday and were prepared for the worst but I am fervently thankful that the youngster is doing well. He was hit by a sniper on the 16th when he went out behind the trenches to explain something to the Major. He was shot through the bladder and, of course, he has a long road of illness and convalescence to go before he can be fit for any duty again.

Yours very truly,
G.A. Cave Orme.

. . . .

The Blind leading the blind

Aug 24th 1915.
Dardenelles.

Dear Colonel Fane,
Progress here has been a bit slower lately. I think it is a case of slow but sure. One often gets little parties of Turks making away from their lines and giving themselves up as prisoners. They seem to know that they'll be well treated as, at first, the prisoners taken were always in an awful fright making sure they would be shot. A very large number of Turcos seem to be employed entirely as labourers to do all the digging everywhere quite apart from the fighting men, really a very sensible idea where they cannot train and equip anything like all. Such a large number of our armed and trained men have to be employed in labourer's work (fatigues) that we could easily do with a special gang of coolies to replace them. Perhaps we shall get some Gippies for the purpose later on but the trouble is they don't like us putting them under fire and there is nowhere here that is not under fire of some sort. The flies are jolly bad here now. One has to wear muslins over ones head like any bit of meat; it looks funny. Ones respirator is useful on certain occasions but not on account of gas poisoning as the Turks don't

use it. It's funny how our ideas about washing change under force of circumstances. I used to imagine myself extraordinary grubby if ever I missed my morning bath but, here, one is lucky if one gets water to wash ones hands and face once a day. The saving grace is the sea where one can go and get clean about every 3rd or 4th day with luck. In some cases though, it is too far off and takes too long to get to a bathing beach. It's always an adventure because the wily Abdul loves having a shot at you when you are in a natural state. Every now and then a thunder storm comes over and is keenly resented as there is no cover from the rain, What we shall do when the rain starts in earnest, I can't imagine but something, with certainty has to be done or else they will all go sick. Those who see service in France have no idea of the lack of conveniences out here. The men have no great coats and no blankets. There are no ambulance wagons let alone huts, no covering material of any kind such as tarpaulins or corrugated iron. How we shall get on in the winter, I really don't know. The more one sees of the campaign, the more one sees of the evil of our policy of muddling through.

I shall be most grateful for any cheap books or paper,

Yours etc,

Weston Amcotts.

....

2nd October 1915   2nd Battalion,
                                                              B.E.F.

Dear Colonel Fane,

I am delighted to say I have got back to my old Battalion and found them all very fit and not a bit depressed about the biff the other day. They took the first two lines of the Bosch defences and hung on for 12 hours when they were bombed out again but it was only supposed to be a demonstration to keep the reserves there. Poor Hopkins was killed just by the third line, I am afraid by one of our own shells. He had been asked not to go too far ahead but was too brave and, on getting over his parapet made straight for Berlin. We lost six killed and four wounded but Griffin, one of them, is only slightly wounded and back on duty and French isn't at all bad but has gone home. The company Commanders are Barker, Griffin, Pitt and Freeman. I am doing 2nd in command as Greatwood was also hit.

We seem to have a splendid lot of men here but could do with some older N.C.O.s It's very peaceful here at the moment so if anyone wants a rest cure, send them here,

Yrs very sincerely,

Reggy Bastard.

....

In billets.

10th december 1915

My Dear Colonel,

We have been having a quiet time since the attack on Sep 28th doing ordinary trench work, four days on and four days in Brigade reserve, rather weary work.

The Germans have been mining up regular. We went off to the 10th Brigade, 3rd Division. I can't pretend we liked it much but it gave one an insight into the new army, I think the general opinion is what might be expected. The men are good but the officers ignorant and the N.C.O,s very poor.

We are getting square again. It takes a long time after a straff to get the Battalion really good again. My own Company was very good before the 28th of September and I hope will be again although I lost some good men.

In the attack the other day, the men were wonderfully steady. At least twice during the day things looked very like a stampeding but, on each occasion, neither was the men's fault.

We were able to hold them easily and the final withdrawal was entirely orderly so much so that I think we only lost about 2 men although we had to cross about 200 yards of country to get to our own lines.

Amongst the many men who died, Lt Corporal Carey, 3rd Batt, stands out. He and Leslie cleared 50 yards of trench with the bayonet. While Leslie went back for his bombs, Carey continued his mad career and captured 18 men on his own. I should have asked the C.O. to send in his name for a V.C. but the poor fellow was killed soon afterwards. His action was at a most critical moment and was of the utmost value. There were army others of the 3rd Battalion who did good work but, as all the men were good, it is difficult to specialise. All the subalterns I had with me were good.

The weather here is terrible now in the trenches, very wet with muck up to the knees.

Please give my love to Massingberd and Milnes,

Yrs very sincerley,

M. Barker

....

15 November 1915

Dear Major Newbury,

We changed our billets yesterday and came a few miles nearer the firing line. We expect to go into the trenches very soon. About the Regiment, we came into action on September 25th and came out on the 27th. We lost over half of the men and 22 officers, killed, missing or wounded..

Captain Stromquist was killed. Captain Harrison, Lt Haldwell, Mather, Rowcroft and Gregg are wounded. Alcock and Hall are prisoners. J.H.R. Manning, Van Somerson and Jacobs are missing. Captain Walton, Capt Topham and Major Storer are missing and believed to be wounded. Coates is supposed to be gassed and is missing. Captain Davis, A.W. Bosworth, Reynolds, Faulkner, Parker and Walsh, we know nothing about. Pattinson, Ken Taylor and myself are the only old hands left. We have now a Major Wilson in command from the 2nd Batt.

We are now resting in billets to get reorganised and equipped. The fight was a very hot one and it was trying for the men who never knew what trenches were or what firing was. We were all taken by surprise when we were suddenly extended out and found the Germans in front of us next morning. We had just done a twelve mile march. We had no water or food but the good old 8th stuck to it. They did good work too. I don't know to this day how I escaped but, thank God, I am alive and very fit,

Yours very sincerely,

Peter Preston

....

Suvla   17th December 1915

Dear Colonel,

I haven't had much chance of writing since we landed here on the first instance. We had a very pleasant journey and were, luckily, unmolested by submarines.

We stayed on the ship at the base from Monday until Tuesday week which was rather boring. On arrival here we went straight up to the trenches. I am 2nd in command. Colonel Hill of the Devon Yeomanry is commanding but I was told that shortly I was to have Colonel Hutchinson who joined up with me at Liverpool.

We had a rather sticky bit of the line to hold and were only 60 to 80 yards from the Turks trenches in rather a nasty salient round which they had snipers posts quite close up to our entanglements. We had the bad luck to have three officers killed and four wounded all in one company in 5 nights, chiefly by snipers and machine guns which wanted our working parties. We are now in a rather less exposed part of the line and fairly comfortable. We came in for a certain amount of shelling but it doesn't do much harm.

Unlike France, where you can get right back when in reserve, here one always comes in for a good deal of shelling. We had a very bad three days just before I got here, rain followed by a blizzard and snow, then it froze hard and was still freezing for a couple of days after I got here, now it is quite nice, fine summer days but rather cold at nights.

One of the first fellows that I met whom I knew was Lambert. I met him at the Marble Arch, i.e, the observation post in our support trenches. He is quite fit and came to tea with us the other day in our Battalion headquarters dug out.

Brig. Gen. Hill commanding the 34th Brigade told me the other day he had asked for me to be his Brigade Major but was refused as the General said I was shortly to take over command of his Battalion.

I am feeling quite fit out here and consequently quite cheerful which I never did at Grimsby,

Kindest remembrances and best wishes for Xmas and the New Year,

Yours sincerely,

G. Kingsley Butt

. . . .

B.E.F.   26 Feb. 1915

Dear Colonel Fanc,

We left Havre on the 13th morning and, after a very long and tedious journey, reached the somewhere on the 13th afternoon. Le Gros met us at the railhead and he proved himself invaluable. He helped us to get breakfast at two in the afternoon. We were very relieved for we were not able to buy many luxuries at Rouen. After breakfast, we continued our journey in a mess cart. We were in the best of spirits at the prospect of meeting old friends but we soon became very quiet. What with the comfort of a mess cart seat and a rough road and Bosche shells ploughing the same road and not far from us, we felt inclined to take the leave train back to town. Both our minds, I think, were drawn to an air fight which concluded with the enemy retiring without loss. We stopped at a village at 4 o'clock and had tea with a chaplain in a conservatory. I did not like the idea of the conservatory with the anti aircraft guns firing. We continued our journey at six o'clock. Things had become very interesting. Verey lights went up by the score but we did get it when we got near B.H.2. The Bosche sent 4HE and two ground shrapnel. Fortunately it didn't do much harm, only to Collins who was attached to us from the Worcesters. He stopped 7 pieces, one piercing his lung but he's coming along nicely now. Our horse got a bit in his hind leg so the Hun gave us a very warm welcome.

We were in immediate support for one night only and I was jolly glad to get away for my billet got shelled regularly every two hours. We were in Crps reserve for a time after that but I was not with my battalion long when I was sent on a fortnight's course on bombing. I am still attending the course. I have learnt quite a lot. The situation of the school is very unwholesome as we are only a mile from the trenches but, so far, they have not scored a direct hit. The Bosche guns have not been very active of late due to the bad weather. It has snowed for five days and the nights are bitterly cold. One of our staff, a corporal, died from exposure. However we have not had any cases of frost bite yet.

I will be leaving the school on Tuesday when I will be going into the trenches for the first time.

I hear Captain Gauntlett and Colonel Cox have been sent home for good now. There is very little news. We are moderately peaceful in this quarter,

I remain yours sincerely,
W.E.Tolley

2nd Batt, Lincoln Regt . B.E.F.
6 March 1916

Dear Sir,
     Eld and myself arrived here on Sat, 26th Feb. We spent 2 days at Base Depot under canvas with about 5 inches of snow on the ground. I think that we became hardened to the rigours of the climate of this country.

We left the base at 10 p.m. on Thursday and spent the rest of the time travelling around France in a very slow train and did not arrive here until 12 o'clock on Saturday.

We went into the trenches on Tuesday night, 29th, and came out on Saturday, 4th. We had very little to worry about whilst we were there.

The weather was very wet and cold and it rained. On our last night (Friday), it rained for about 3 hours and then snowed for the next twelve. Consequently, the state of the ground was atrocious in the extreme and one was fortunate on finding ground to walk upon that was not worse than Wellsby camp was in November.

Now there are foot-boards to walk on but if one walks off these which is easily possible when there is 6 to 8 inches of water above them as there was on Friday, you usually go down in the mud up to your knees.

We go into the trenches again on Wednesday and I am hoping the weather will have changed for the better by then.

Trusting that you are very well,

I am Your Obedient Servant,

J. Dudley Drysdale.

....

4th Infantry brigade, South Farm,
Chisledon, Wilts.

Dear Colonel,

Many changes have taken place since I have been away from you. I got to Grantham which I found in chaos, owing to the Machine Gun Corps just starting. I think the Corps will be a very big thing when it does get going properly. I get on very well with the staff at Grantham and I was honoured by being picked out to take over the job as Brigade Machine Gun Officer to a Brigade that is going to West Africa. I believe Smith Dorrien is taking us out. We are here getting fitted out. The Brigade is composed of the Volunteer Cycle Corps, 6th Sussex, 9th Hampshires, 1st Kents and 25th London. They seem a very good lot of fellows. I believe McGrath has new staff at Grantham as instructors.

I remain, Yours sincerely,
A. Rickets.

They are making me temporary Captain while I'm on this job

. . . .

11th West Yorkshire Regt. B.E.F.
12 March 1916

My Dear Colonel,
         I took over the Battalion in Reserve at Hazebrook but since then we have been moved down south and have taken over a line from the French near Souchez. Trench conditions are like last winter. We came out 2 nights ago and did not get the men into billets until 5 a.m. all very tired and footsore. We have had a lot of snow lately and the trenches are very wet. This district is quite an education. Going up to the trenches themselves is an education as one goes through the district in which the heavy fighting of last year took place. Souchez, Garrency, Ablain and St Nazaire are merely heaps of stones, the woods cut down and what is left of the trees are left cut about and blackened. The whole of the ground is a mass of shell craters, some of them very big. The line itself is somewhat lively and there is a lot of shelling most of the time. Casualties are not as heavy as one might expect as the ground is chalk and consequently it has been possible to contrive deep dugouts. We await the spring offensive.

Yours very sincerely,
M. Barker.

59

My dear Uncle Will,

I was dining with Buit and he showed me a long letter from you. I am glad you are flourishing in Grimsby. He turned up at Suvla. I met him in the trenches there having previously met him in the Hospital Ship coming from France. All the time we were on the Peninsula, the fighting was very peaceful indeed and, except for the deluge and blizzard in November, the weather very pleasant.

I think Mother must have sent you what news I had about the evacuation. It was a good show of its kind. I wish we could have put the thing through as evacuations, even if successful, are not much to buck about. We were a month in the desert near Cairo and have been here nearly a month collecting our stuff. I have no idea of the next move. I should like a staff job in Mesopotamia myself even if it is a filthy climate, to have a look at the place. This fall of Erzerum must make a difference there though.

We lead a quiet and pleasant life here, not much work, some golf, tennis and today a little boat sailing in and out of the harbour.

I don't know that I can tell you much about trench warfare at Suvla. The only thing that might be of use to your new officers is this – they can only get artillery fire by applying through their C.O. through the brigade and after a devil of a lot of fuss. If they would only come and talk to the local gunner just behind or in their trenches, more likely the latter, they can get anything they like shot at if he has the ammunition and is an ordinary mortal. At Suvla, the officers looked at him as if he was a strange beast and never even thought of passing the time of day with him. I only found out this idea of getting artillery fire through the proper channels today. They also seem to be divided into two classes:

one believes an 18pr can hit a sixpence at 3,000 feet and the other which squeals if one of our own shells comes within a mile of them.

I gather Harry is at Salonica. They seem to be having quiet times there too. I believe Weston Amcotts is in these parts too but I have neither seen nor heard of him,

Your affectionate nephew,
Alex Lambert

．．．．．．．．．．．．．．．．．．

Lincoln
July 11th 1916

My Dear Fane,
The War Office tells me that our boy is missing, July 1st which we hope means that he is alive in the hands of the enemy, not a great comfort considering their treatment of some of their prisoners but better than the worst. I don't know whether any details of the 2nd share in the advance has reached you. If so, you may know more than we are able to find out. I have interviewed two wounded men in the Hospital here but neither of them know much of what happened as they were among the early casualties. Bolam has just been in and tells me that he has seen three more men later arrived and they cannot tell him anything.

The Bishop's youngest son is wounded in the thigh. I hope not seriously. The machine guns seem to have been deadly,

Yours very truly,
G.W. Jeudwine (Archdeacon of Lincoln)

．．．．．．．．．．．．．．．．．．．．．．

2nd Battalion, Lincs Regiment, 8th Division. B.E.F.
15th July 1916

Dear Colonel Fane,

Just a line to thank you for your letter and in anticipation of what you may do for my mother.

About Jeudwine, his people have most probably been informed that he is missing and we have been unable to find any further trace of him. He was commanding V Company who went over on the left of the battalion front with the 70th Brigade on their left. The latter were held up, consequently we came under heavy oblique fire which caused many casualties.

I am now commanding this Company and have had to make a history as far and, as I could gather, both Jeudwine and Shaw got into the first trench alright and endeavoured to lead the men on to the second line according to the plan of attack. Reinforcements could not be brought up owing to the heavy fire and, as both flanks were in the air, the Battalion was forced to retire to the trenches.

There would seem to be a possibility of Jeudwine being made a prisoner but, between ourselves, I'm afraid the Hun was really ratty and was out for blood. I have a pile of letters here for Jeudwine which I am returning to his people.

Griffith had rather an exciting time during the strafe which, together with trouble from his own wound has been too much for him and he has gone down the line.

With kindest regards to yourself and Captain James,
I remain,
Yours truly,
F.W.Clfton

....

Weelsby Camp 1917

2nd Batt, Lincs Regt.

7 July, 1916.

Dear Colonel Fane,

My younger brother is on his way home to enlist so I am writing to ask if you would look favourably on his application for a Commission. He is 18 and has done a certain amount of training in the Shanghai Volunteer Corps. I don't quite know when he should arrive but he should be back in a fortnight.

The Battalion lost heavily in this last show. Col. Bastard, Major Pitt, Leslie, Drysdale and Griffith are the only ones left. Ingolsby, Major Pitt, Drysdale and I were left behind. Of those that went in, three are left.

With the kindest regards to Mrs Fane and yourself,
Yours sincerely,
F.W. Clifton.

Missing; Jeudwine, Ross,. Shaw, Ckifford.
Killed; Needham, Toolis, Meyer, Austin, Sharp, Aplin, Wiseman.
Wounded; Sowerby, Shearman, Gates, Carter (uncertain), Bennett, Skelby, Eld.

26th July 1916

My Dear Fane,

      I am about beat, as they say, for a R.S.M. Do you think you cold help me? Barker came over to see me yesterday afternoon and said you had a C.S.M. Murphy who would be the very man for the appointment. There is no N.C.O. on this Batt that is fit for the position, they all stand too much in need of instruction themselves. A really smart man and good disciplinarian from some other unit as R.S.M. would improve them enormously. We are still out but expect to go up again any day now and, from all accounts, one may expect a fairly warm time when we get there. Senior officers especially are saying that commanders of experience are very badly needed out here. I have hardly got any and am very short of officers altogether.

      Very seriously yours,
      E Kyme Cordeaux

....

Somerville Hospital, Oxford.
18/7/16

Dear Colonel Fane,

      I can give you some information regarding the time and place of attack on the 2nd and 19th Batts. I can give none regarding any of the officers reported missing,

      I have received letters of enquiry from Lady Clifford and Mrs Shaw but neither I nor any of the others in this hospital saw anything of their sons during the attack. The 2nd Batt attacked the left of the village of Ovillers at 7.30.a.m. on the 1st July and, although the German second line trench was reached by a few men, the battalion was so reduced and the Germans were too strong at this point that we had to withdraw less than a company strong. The following officers went into the attack.

W Company; Griffiths, Ross, Appelin, Stevens (Devons)

X Coy; Needham, Toolis, Skilly, Woodcock.
Y Coy: Jeudwine, Shaw, Sowerby, Jennuett
Z Coy: Wiseman. Shearman, Gates, Meyer, Austey.
Clifford was in G.O.
Ferguson J.M. Battery
Drysdale in Bde Bombers,.

I was with X Coy but was wounded the night before when cutting our own wire, the Colonel, the Adj, Griffiths, Fergusson, Ingoldsby and Major Pitts are the only ones that have come through scot free. The last two being in reserve.

The 19th Batt on our right who were in the 34th Div attacked at the same time in the vicinity of La Boiselle and I believe had a lot of casualties. Sowerby is badly knocked about but I believe his case is not serious and he will recover in time.

Skelly's and Barrett's wounds are painful but they are both progressing favourably. My wound is practically healed and I am able to get about a little. The following officers are in this hospital, Marshall, Bruce, Barrett, Robinson, Hanning, Sowerby, Skelly, Woodcock and myself. There are also some officers from the 8th and 10th Batt whose names I do not know. I expect I shall be joining up with you in the next two months,

Yours sincerely,
A.W. Eld

. . . .

22 December 1916   6th Lincs Regt.

Dear Colonel Fane,

I am writing a few lines to wish you and everyone at the Old Batt a merry Christmas and a happy New Year. I wish I was going to be there with you all as Christmas for me is not looking very cheery.

Since I last wrote to you, I have travelled considerably. I joined the Batt when they were resting and I had a fortnight like that. Then they started marching and carried on for a week like that. Then our company got sent off for a day's grave digging and fetching in the dead. It was a very gruesome job. The next day we went in the line for nine days and had a very rough journey. I got hit on the last day but was not bad enough to go to the doctor but it was very sore and uncomfortable. I was jolly lucky. It was a quiet shell and landed only four feet from me. I hope my luck will last.

I am away from the Batt now in charge of a working party with another officer and a hundred men from three different Regiments. We are helping the R.E.s with a light railway. Unfortunately we are not billeted decently but are in the reserve lines of the German dug outs about a mile in front of our work. It is not a very savoury place. My dugout is about 30 feet deep but it is very cold and the water comes in everywhere and the rats and mice are a perfect plague. I have been here ten days now and am here for another ten. The Battalion came in five days ago and go out again in three days time. I think we'll be back with them just in time for the next which will mean I've been a month with only two days break but I suppose one must say 'C'est la Guerre'.

Was that Sub Lt Fane that won the D.S.O. any relation of yours? I thought he would be older than your son who is in the navy.

I have got my papers complete for the Indian Army and they have started their travels so I suppose I will hear something about March.

With best wishes for Xmas and the coming year,
W.S. Barroll

....

27 December 1916.   B.E.F. Port Said.

Dear Colonel Fane,
                As you can see I am at Port Said where I
have been carrying on the duty of Base Censor for some time.
While I was alone, the work was very hard but now that there are
three of us, there is very little to do. Things have been very quiet
here and I would give anything to be back in France and back
with the Battalion. I am perfectly fit and sound for duty and
besides all my interests are with the Lincolns. Would it be
possible for me to be fetched back to do some fighting instead of
this? This is an excellent job for an unfit person. I don't want you
to think I'm grousing but I want to be back with the Regiment in
France.
            It has been very hot out here all winter, Xmas day being
very hot. Today is the first wet day since February.
            My very best wishes for the New Year and I hope it may be
possible for me to be fetched back to the Regiment.
                        Yours sincerely,
                        J.W.F.Mayer

                ………………………………

                                    Lady Dudley's Home, Brighton
                                    Feb 8, 1917

My Dear Colonel Fane,
                I must thank you for your enquiries since I was
unfortunately wounded. I say unfortunately but I think really that I
have been very lucky in that I was not given 'out' altogether.
They tell me I have put up rather a wonderful show in the way of
recovering, though this really is no credit to me. The abdominal
wound is going on splendidly but I have not, as yet, done
anything in the way of stairs. I walk about the room a bit but I will

know more about my legs when I have had a chance to test them properly. The place where the left tibia was broken is low down and just above the ankle. I have several small bits of bone in my leg that will have to come out I expect and in several places, the muscle has disappeared for the time being but this is only natural since I have nine wounds in each leg. My little finger was broken too but that is alright now.

We are very well looked after here and the air is positively grand. I received a communication from the War Office the other day to say that a medical board had granted me leave from Jan 10th to April 12th. This place is now recognised as a Red Cross Auxiliary Hospital. Last time when I was here, Lady Ancaster was defraying all expenses. (The Home then took fourteen patients). She very generously did so for six months.

Perhaps I better tell you how I came to be wounded. I was making sure that proper contact was going to be kept up between my company's extreme left of the Brigade and the extreme right of the Battalion on our left. It was 10.30 at night. The intermediate trenches are not held by day but by bombing posts at night. I was going along with my sergeant, as I often had before, over this ground which was quite churned up with mortar fire when we were challenged by a frightened voice. I replied quite loudly and reassuringly and the words were hardly out of my mouth when a Mills Bomb burst at our feet. They were evidently very nervous about being raided. They had no justification for their supposing we were any threat.

The sergeant was going on well the last I heard of him at McCar Clearing Station.

I was sorry to hear of Bennett's death He was such a cheery fellow under any circumstance and looked like making a good soldier. You will have heard how he was shot by one of our own sentries on Xmas Eve. I gather he had been pretty busy with trench mortaring and that he had already been buried earlier on in the day. He was wearing a soft cap and, on the sentry challenging him, he tripped up and the sentry shot him dead

I wonder what you think of the war now, Sir? It seems to me that the Huns have all their cards on the table, face up.
Hoping this finds you well in this terribly cold weather,
Yours very sincerely,
Neil J. Edmondson.

Feb 26

Lincs Regt
A.P.O.S10
B.E.F.

Dear Will,

I was very glad to see your name in the list today. It is some slight recognition of all the work you have done during the last two and a half years.

I was ordered away from the 1st Battalion early in January when they were out at the back of the front line for a month on 5 weeks leave which they thoroughly deserved and sent off on a L of C job as being too old and inexperienced in trench warfare to stay on the front line. I was sorry to leave the Batt but I can't honestly say that I am sorry that I did not go back to the trenches which I found a singularly unattractive mode of living. The perpetual semi darkness of the dug outs and hardly being able to stand up straight in them, the cramped space and the mud and the rats and the paucity of washing facilities to say nothing of the Boche trench mortar bombs made existence in the trenches thoroughly uncomfortable and unpleasant and I felt like a released prisoner when we came out.

I went to Calais and was put in charge of a rest camp just outside the town which had been pitched on a swamp, so it was in a jolly state after all the rain we had had before the frost set in. However, the camp did not last long. It was abolished. All the tents were struck and, with all the camp equipment returned to ordnance, I was moved on here, 20 miles from Calais and some 15 miles from the front line. I was rather pleased that the C.O. Brigadier and the Divisional General asked that I might say on with the 1st Batt but G.H.Q. or whoever it is that finally settles these things would not allow it.

I have been here a month and have a large camp of 2,400 men, none of them fighting troops but employed on various L of C jobs. They are a dirty lot of scallywags and among them is a labour Batt commanded by Col. Searle who was at Brocklesby and who greeted me as an old friend. The camp had only just been started when I came so there has been a good deal to do, improvising baths, washing and sanitary arrangements and laboriously constructing dugouts for the camp as we have had German aeroplanes over and one or two casualties from bombs dropped by them. I sleep in a room in a cottage close to the camp. The officers are not numerous, a job lot you might say.

I hope you have good news of Harry,

Yours sincerely,

Stephen Massingberd.

70

1st March

Dear Colonel,

I was delighted to see your name in the honours list and congratulate you heartily. I am acting as 2nd in Command here as Massingberd is away and Orr has gone back to one of the schools. I hope to be gazetted temporary major shortly unless Elkingtom turns up but I think this unlikely. The men surprised me agreeably. I think they are a good, steady lot, much above the average as regards their physique. We are getting a new Colonel, someone from the Black Watch I believe. It's difficult to find N.C.O.s for sergeants. If Disbrowe could let us know when some good ones are coming up, we'll try and get them sent to us by applying to the base.

Yours sincerely,
G.W. Wales

………………………………

8 March 1917   2 Lincs Regt. B.E.F.

Dear Colonel Fane,

I thought it might interest you to know that the 8th Div had, at last, carried out a successful attack. We had to find the moppers up consisting of C Corps which I had the honour of commanding, also a carrying party composing of B Coy. The attack was on the big ground in front of Moistanes and was carried out on a two Brigade frontage, the Berks representing the 25th Brigade.

The taking of the position was simple as the Boche did not show much fight but his bombardment later was pretty heavy. Casualties were fairly small we losing in officers, one killed

(Grantham), missing – Cocks and 2 wounded – Galpin and Nichols. This took place on the 4th and here we are back in the line holding the position, rather different to earlier days in which, after a show, we had 3 weeks rest. Skerrington was wounded last night in the neck.

We are all pleased to hear you were amongst those mentioned by the Secretary of War Honours List.
Congratulations
By the way, Eld has rejoined us.
Trusting you are well,
Yours sincerely,
F.W. Clifton.

....